COME FOLLOW ME
ACTIVITY BOOK FOR KIDS
THE BOOK OF MORMON

2024

TWO ACTIVITY PAGES FOR EVERY WEEKLY LESSON FOR THE ENTIRE YEAR OF 2024

ABOUT THIS BOOK

This is an activity book for kids ages 6-11 that goes along with the weekly Come, Follow Me curriculum. Each week has two activity pages to complete. Enjoy!

THIS BOOK BELONGS TO:

_____

LESSON SCHEDULE

January

Jan 1-7	Intro Pages
Jan 8-14	1 Nephi 1-5
Jan 15-21	1 Nephi 6-10
Jan 22-28	1 Nephi 11-15

February

Jan 29-Feb 4	1 Nephi 16-22
Feb 5-11	2 Nephi 1-2
Feb 12-18	2 Nephi 3-5
Feb 19-25	2 Nephi 6-10

March

Feb 26-Mar 3	2 Nephi 11-19
Mar 4-10	2 Nephi 20-25
Mar 11-17	2 Nephi 26-30
Mar 18-24	2 Nephi 31-33
Mar 25-31	Easter

April

April 1-7	Jacob 1-4
April 8-14	Jacob 5-7
April 15-21	Enos-Words Mormon
April 22-28	Mosiah 1-3

May

April 29-May 5	Mosiah 4-6
May 6-12	Mosiah 7-10
May 13-19	Mosiah 11-17
May 20-26	Mosiah 18-24

June

May 27-Jun 2	Mosiah 25-28
Jun 3-9	Mosiah 29-Alma 4
Jun 10-16	Alma 5-7
Jun 17-23	Alma 8-12
Jun 24-30	Alma 13-16

July

Jul 1-7	Alma 17-22
Jul 8-14	Alma 23-29
Jul 15-21	Alma 30-31
Jul 22-28	Alma 32-35

August

Jul 29-Aug 4	Alma 36-38
Aug 5-11	Alma 39-42
Aug 12-18	Alma 43-52
Aug 19-25	Alma 53-63

September

Aug 26-Sept 1	Helaman 1-6
Sept 2-8	Helaman 7-12
Sept 9-15	Helaman 13-16
Sept 16-22	3 Nephi 1-7
Sept 23-29	3 Nephi 8-11

October

Sept 30-Oct 6	3 Nephi 12-16
Oct 7-13	3 Nephi 17-19
Oct 14-20	3 Nephi 20-26
Oct 21-27	3 Nephi 27-4 Nephi

November

Oct 28-Nov 3	Mormon 1-6
Nov 4-10	Mormon 7-9
Nov 11-17	Ether 1-5
Nov 18-24	Ether 6-11

December

Nov 25-Dec 1	Ether 12-15
Dec 2-8	Moroni 1-6
Dec 9-15	Moroni 7-9
Dec 16-22	Moroni 10
Dec 23-29	Christmas

MY GOALS FOR THIS YEAR

Write or draw your spiritual, physical, social, and intellectual goals for this year below.

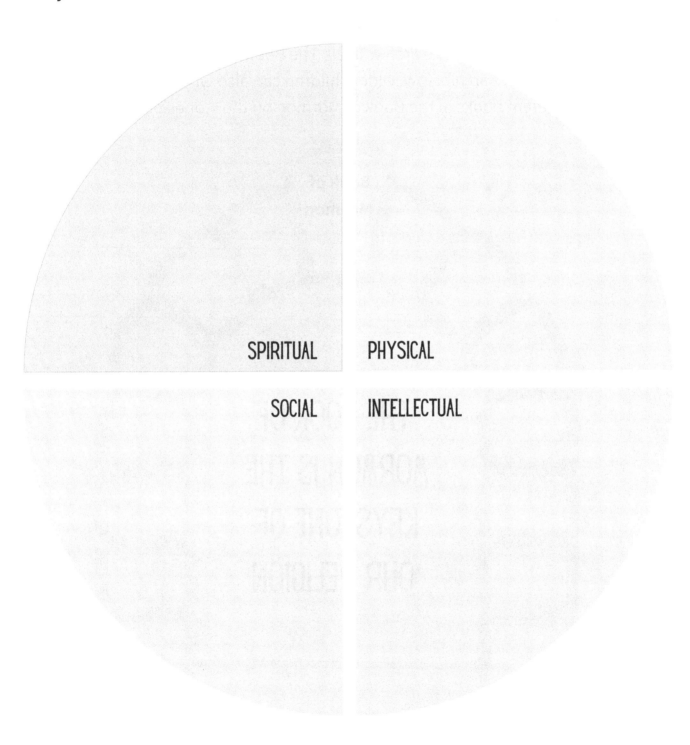

SPIRITUAL

PHYSICAL

SOCIAL

INTELLECTUAL

JANUARY 1-7

A keystone is a central stone at the top of the arch that holds the arch together. If the keystone is removed, the whole arch will fall. The Book of Mormon is the keystone of our doctrine. Color the arch below. Older children can also write all the names of the different books in the Book of Mormon on the stones below.

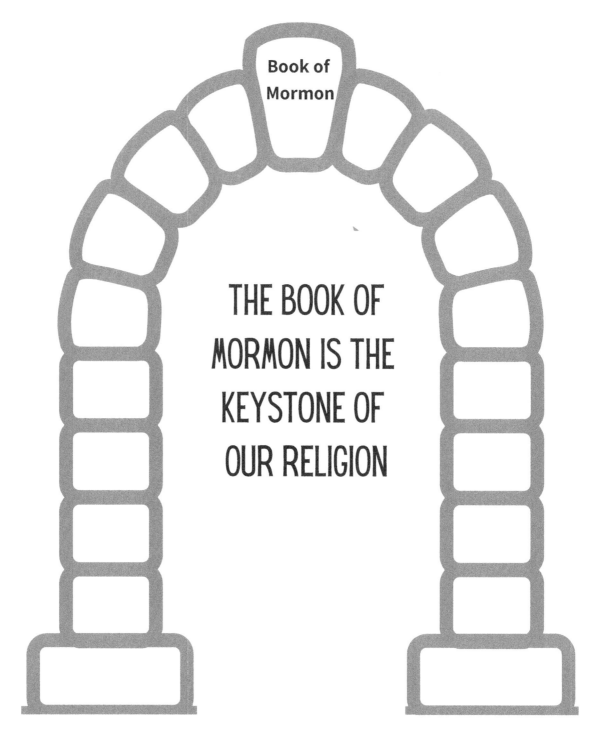

INTRODUCTORY PAGES OF THE BOOK OF MORMON

As you study the Book of Mormon this year, it is first important to learn the history of how we got the book. Match each statement below to the correct picture. Color the pictures.

JOSEPH SMITH TRANSLATED THE GOLD PLATES & PUBLISHED THE BOOK OF MORMON

ANGEL TOLD JOSEPH SMITH WHERE TO FIND THE PLATES

JOSEPH SMITH PRAYED & ASKED WHICH CHURCH TO JOIN - THIS STARTED THE RESTORATION OF GOSPEL

A RECORD & TESTIMONY OF JESUS CHRIST BY THE PEOPLE LIVING IN THE AMERICAS ANCIENTLY

MORONI BURIED THE GOLD PLATES

JANUARY 8-14

Nephi had great faith and was willing to "go and do" the things the Lord commanded (see 1 Nephi 3:7). Nephi knew the Lord would help him. On the arrows below, color all the words that rhyme with "do" to remind you to always "do" what the Lord asks.

RHYME TIME: WORDS THAT RHYME WITH "DO"

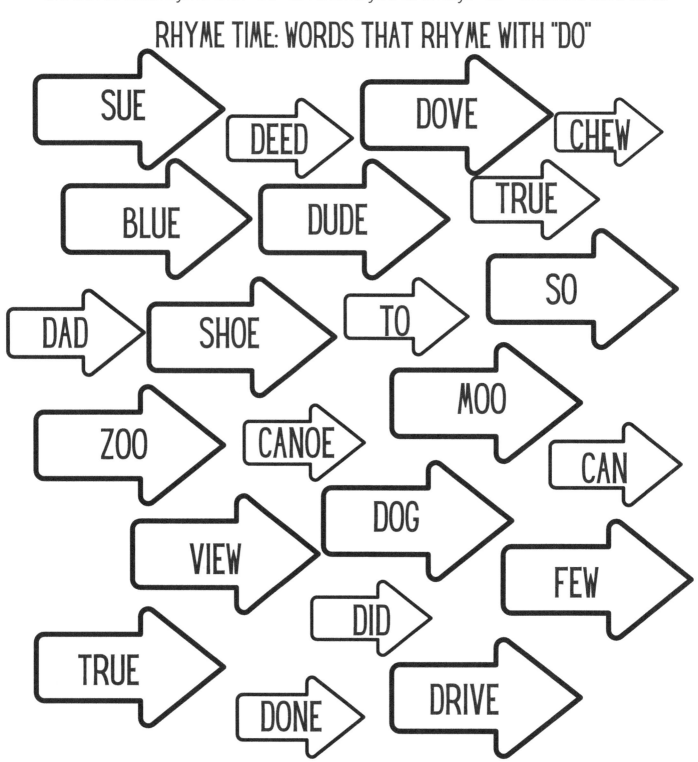

1 NEPHI 1-5

The scriptures were very important to Lehi & his family. Nephi & his brothers traveled a great distance to go back to Jerusalem and get the brass plates from Laban. Complete the maze below and help Nephi get the brass plates.

NEPHI IN WILDERNESS

LABAN & BRASS PLATES IN JERUSALEM

JANUARY 15-21

Lehi's vision teaches the importance of "holding to the rod" and following God's word. Color the picture below. Draw yourself holding onto the rod.

HOLD TO THE ROD

1 NEPHI 6-10

Heavenly Father gave Lehi a dream to teach Lehi and his family how to gain happiness. Each of the objects in the dream had a special meaning. Read 1 Nephi chapter 8 with your family or primary class to learn about the dream. Match the object with its meaning below.

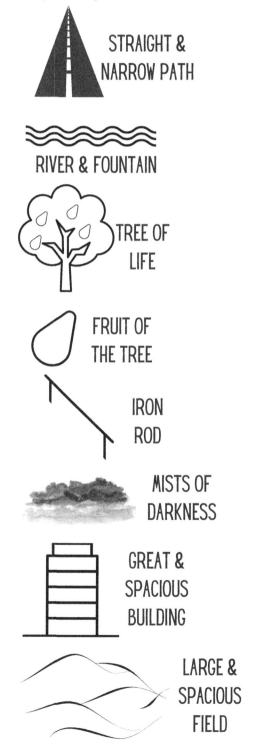

STRAIGHT & NARROW PATH

RIVER & FOUNTAIN

TREE OF LIFE

FRUIT OF THE TREE

IRON ROD

MISTS OF DARKNESS

GREAT & SPACIOUS BUILDING

LARGE & SPACIOUS FIELD

THE WORLD

BLESSINGS THAT COME THROUGH THE SAVIOR'S ATONEMENT

SATAN'S INFLUENCE IN WORLD/DEPTHS OF HELL

WORD OF GOD

OBEDIENCE TO THE COMMANDEMENTS OF GOD

TEMPTATIONS OF SATAN

PRIDEFUL& UNKIND PEOPLE WHO MOCK OTHERS

LOVE OF GOD

JANUARY 22-28

In 1 Nephi 13:26–29, 35–36, 40, we learn that the Book of Mormon teaches us precious truths that were lost from the bible over time. Complete the activity below.

PLAIN AND PRECIOUS TRUTHS

HOW MANY WORDS CAN YOU MAKE USING THE LETTERS FROM WORDS ABOVE "PLAIN AND PRECIOUS TRUTHS"?

_____   _____

_____   _____

_____   _____

_____   _____

_____   _____

_____   _____

_____

1 NEPHI 11-15

Nephi was shown events from Jesus' life, including his birth. Trace the picture below of baby Jesus.

TRACE IT!

In 1 Nephi 17:7–19; 18:1–4, the Lord commands Nephi to build a boat for his family to sail to the promised land. Nephi had never done this before, so he relied on the Lord. The Lord helps us with difficult things in our lives. Below, draw a picture of what you think Nephi's boat looked like.

NEPHI BUILT A BOAT

1 NEPHI 16-22

The Lord gave Lehi and his family the Liahona to guide them. The Liahona only worked when they obeyed God. Complete the word search below containing words from this week's reading.

```
E  O  W  N  C  E  L  P  M  A  X  E
M  T  A  N  O  H  A  I  L  W  N  X
A  D  X  N  M  U  B  P  T  K  Z  N
G  F  G  Z  M  F  Y  N  C  W  Q  N
N  F  M  D  A  E  E  W  O  K  S  S
K  G  P  N  N  I  C  B  M  X  G  O
K  K  Q  E  D  I  M  O  P  S  K  L
M  A  P  E  M  X  S  C  A  E  P  E
X  H  B  Y  E  Y  N  H  S  D  A  X
I  O  E  W  N  L  I  D  S  I  I  D
K  H  Q  E  T  E  Z  V  V  U  X  I
L  J  E  Y  S  E  T  B  W  G  N  E
```

COMPASS	MAP	LIAHONA
COMMANDMENTS	GUIDES	NEPHI
EXAMPLE	OBEDIENT	BOW

FEBRUARY 5-11

In 2 Nephi 2:11, 16, 27, Lehi teaches his family that there must be opposition in all things. We could never know joy if we didn't know pain. Agency is part of God's plan for us here on Earth. Color the pictures below and match the opposites.

In 2 Nephi 2, Lehi teaches that Adam and Eve partaking of the forbidden fruit made it possible for all of us on Earth to have the gift of agency. We can choose good or evil. Crack the code to find a message from this week's lesson.

CRACK THE CODE

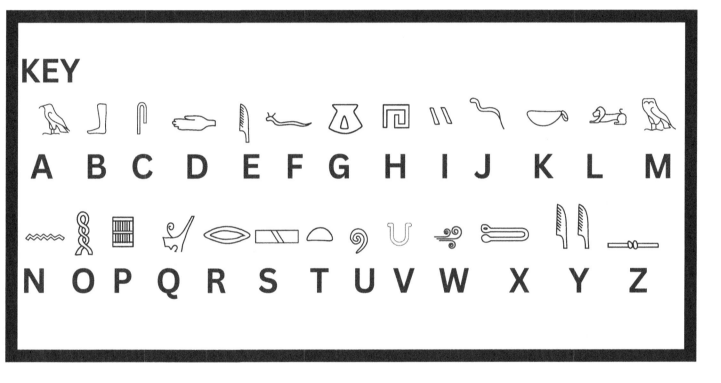

KEY

A B C D E F G H I J K L M

N O P Q R S T U V W X Y Z

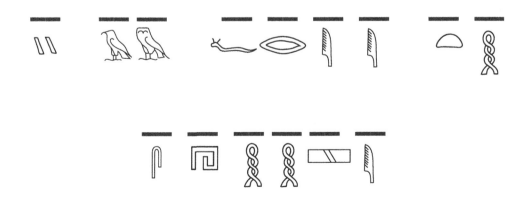

FEBRUARY 12-18

CIRCLE THE DAYS YOU READ THIS WEEK: MON TUES WED THUR FRI SAT SUN

In 2 Nephi 3:6, we learn about a "choice seer," who we now know was Joseph Smith. A seer is someone who has the gift from God of being able to see spiritually. Below color all the eyes with words that rhyme with "seer."

RHYME TIME: WORDS THAT RHYME WITH "SEER"

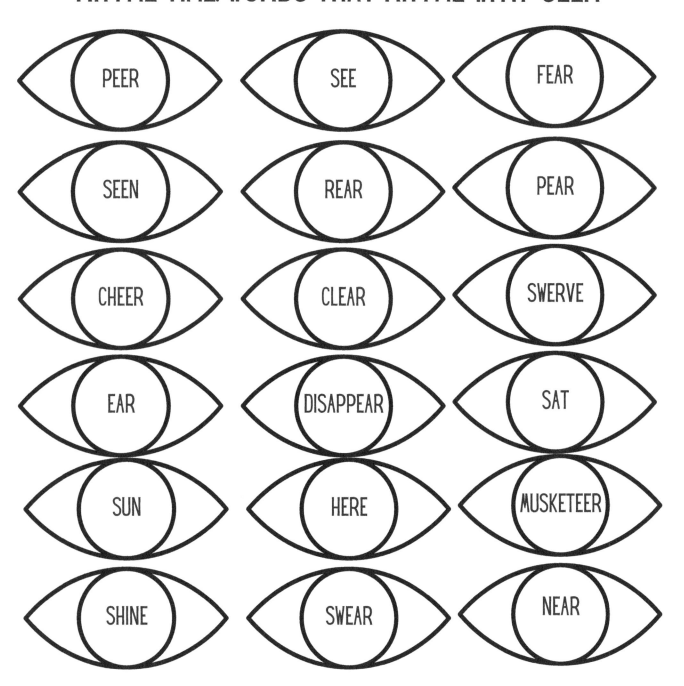

2 NEPHI 3-5

In 2 Nephi 5:15–16, Nephi builds a temple. What is special about temples? In the box below, draw a picture of what you think Nephi's temple looked like.

TEMPLES ARE HOUSES OF THE LORD

FEBRUARY 19-25

In 2 Nephi 9:6–10, 19–24, we learn Jesus is our Savior, as well as the importance of His atonement. Pick the correct entrance to the word search below to find your way to Christ.

WHICH ENTRANCE IS CORRECT?

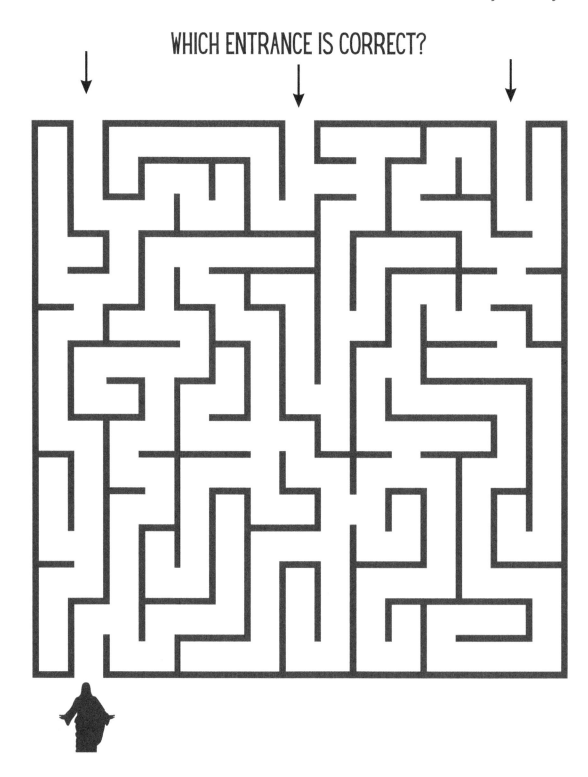

In 2 Nephi 9:49, we learn to let our hearts "delight" in righteousness and to praise God. In the hearts below, write or draw good "righteous" choices you can make.

"MY HEART DELIGHTETH IN RIGHTEOUSNESS"

FEBRUARY 26-MARCH 3

CIRCLE THE DAYS YOU READ THIS WEEK: MON TUES WED THUR FRI SAT SUN

In 2 Nephi 12:2–3, Isaiah teaches us why we have temples. Complete the word search below with words related to the temple.

I LOVE TO SEE THE TEMPLE

```
C  F  E  W  O  J  U  H  C  E  U
N  W  E  T  U  T  I  O  L  I  C
J  N  Q  O  E  L  P  M  E  T  R
M  I  Q  K  S  R  L  O  W  Q  D
U  A  I  G  E  M  N  T  H  L  Q
U  T  R  B  A  P  T  I  S  M  S
L  N  X  R  L  C  S  H  T  G  Z
E  U  K  Y  I  D  R  O  L  Y  Y
J  O  H  V  N  A  G  U  X  L  X
E  M  P  H  G  J  G  S  Q  X  Q
B  Y  V  I  S  D  K  E  Q  G  Q
```

TEMPLE	ETERNITY	BAPTISMS
SEALINGS	MARRIAGE	HOUSE
LORD	MOUNTAIN	

2 NEPHI 11-19

Throughout the scriptures, many names are given to Jesus. In 2 Nephi 11:4–7; 17:14; 19:6, some of those names are listed. Color the names of Christ below and discuss with your family or primary class what those names mean.

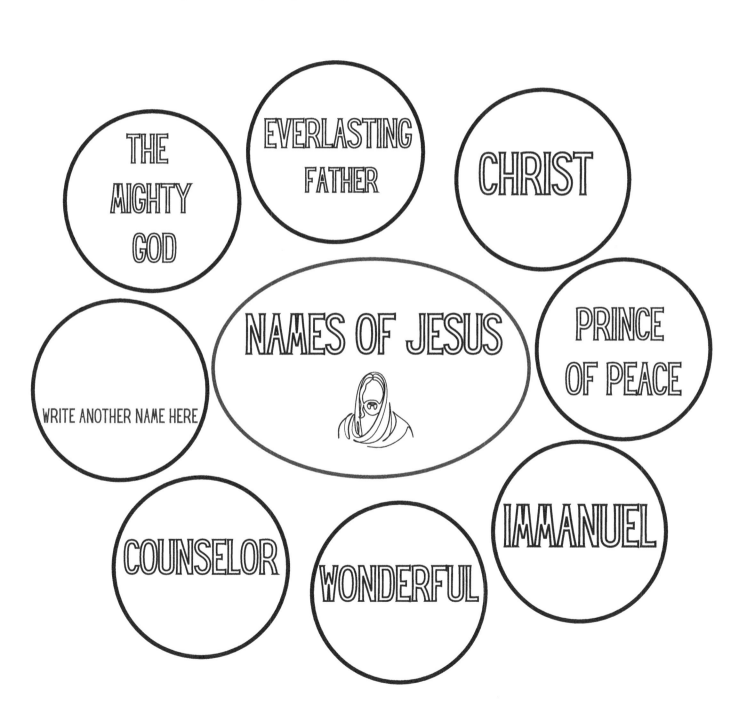

THE MIGHTY GOD

EVERLASTING FATHER

CHRIST

NAMES OF JESUS

PRINCE OF PEACE

WRITE ANOTHER NAME HERE

COUNSELOR

WONDERFUL

IMMANUEL

MARCH 4-10

In 2 Nephi 21:11–12, we learn the Lord is gathering His people and setting up an "ensign for the nations." On the flag below, draw pictures and and write words to represent your testimony & what you love about the Gospel of Christ.

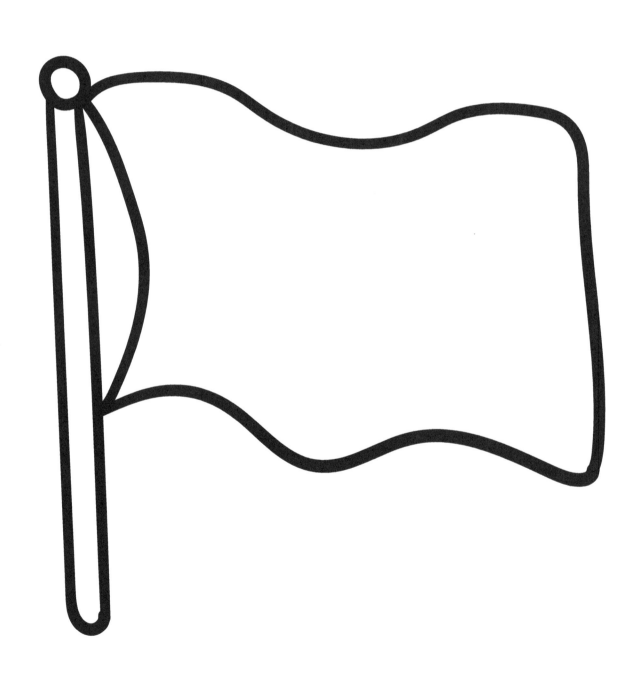

In 2 Nephi 25:26, we learn about "rejoicing" in Christ. Fill in the missing words in the scripture below and see if you can memorize the scripture.

"AND WE _____OF CHRIST, WE _____IN CHRIST, WE _____OF CHRIST, WE _____OF CHRIST, AND WE WRITE ACCORDING TO OUR PROPHECIES, THAT OUR _____MAY KNOW TO WHAT SOURCE THEY MAY LOOK FOR A REMISSION OF THEIR _____."

CHILDREN PROPHESY SINS REJOICE TALK
PREACH

MARCH 11-17

CIRCLE THE DAYS YOU READ THIS WEEK: MON TUES WED THUR FRI SAT SUN

In 2 Nephi 26:23–28, 33, Jesus invites everyone to come unto Him and partake of His goodness and salvation. Invite a friend to "come unto Christ" and decorate and fill out the invite below and decorate.

YOU ARE INVITED
TO COME UNTO CHRIST!

TO: ________

FROM: ________

In 2 Nephi 28:2, we learn the Book of Mormon is of "great worth" to us. In the gift below, write or draw why the Book of Mormon is important to you.

THE BOOK OF MORMON IS A GIFT & BLESSING TO ME

MARCH 18-24

In 2 Nephi 31, Nephi tells us the steps we need to take to receive eternal life. Write or draw some of the steps below on the stepping stones. Some examples include being baptized, receiving the Holy Ghost, keeping the commandments, repenting, etc.

STEPS TO ETERNAL LIFE

2 NEPHI 31-33

In 2 Nephi 32:3–5, we are taught to feast upon the words of Christ. Color all of the synonyms of the word "feast" on the dinner plates below.

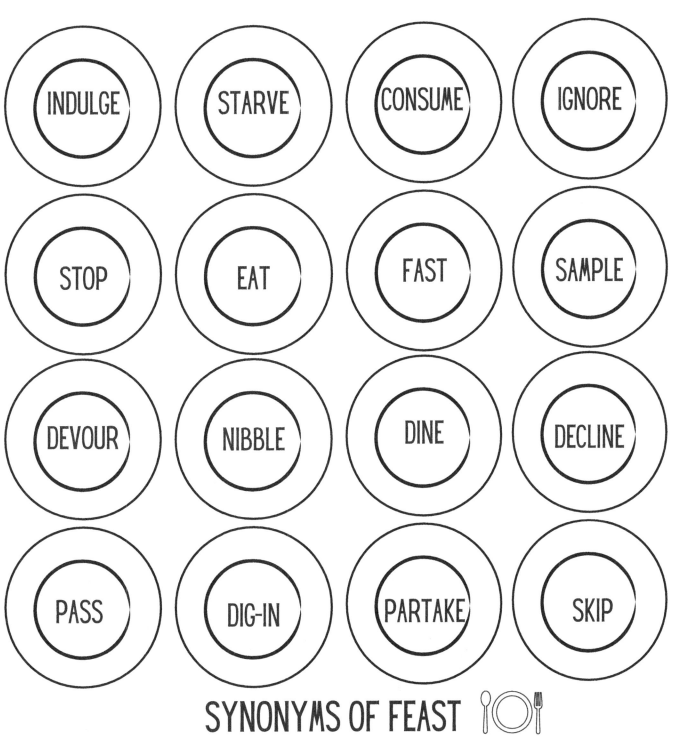

INDULGE   STARVE   CONSUME   IGNORE

STOP   EAT   FAST   SAMPLE

DEVOUR   NIBBLE   DINE   DECLINE

PASS   DIG-IN   PARTAKE   SKIP

SYNONYMS OF FEAST

MARCH 25-31

Because of Jesus, we all will be resurrected and live again. Because of Jesus, we can also repent of our sins and be forgiven. Complete the maze below and choose the correct entrance to get to center of egg.

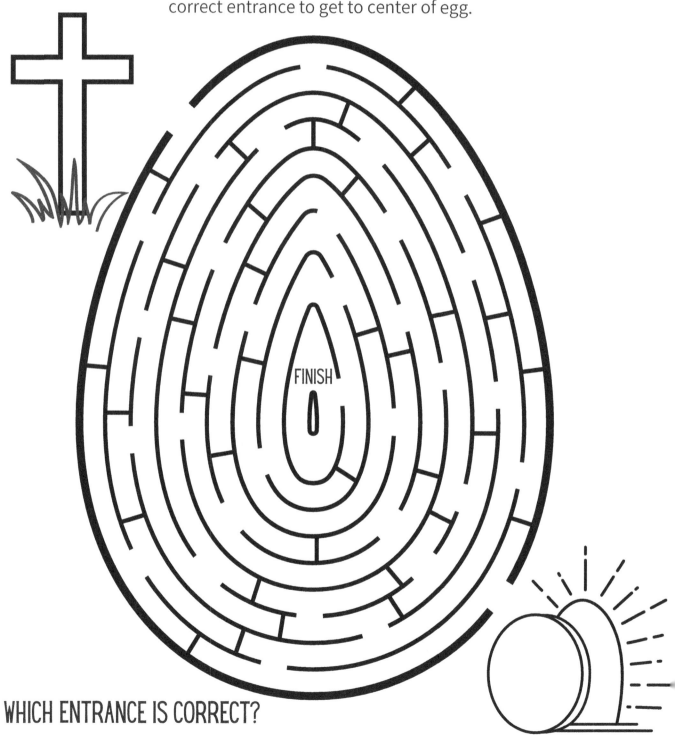

FINISH

WHICH ENTRANCE IS CORRECT?

EASTER

Jesus was resurrected and we will be, too. See how many words you can make from the words "Jesus was resurrected."

JESUS WAS RESURRECTED

HOW MANY WORDS CAN YOU MAKE USING THE LETTERS FROM WORDS ABOVE "JESUS WAS RESURRECTED"?

_____   _____

_____   _____

_____   _____

_____   _____

_____   _____

_____   _____

_____   _____

_____

APRIL 1-7

Jacob was Nephi's brother. He testified to the people about Christ and gave them warnings. Complete the word search below.

```
Y  F  I  T  S  E  T  S  J  U
A  D  T  S  P  S  D  I  N  D
N  H  S  R  I  R  L  S  I  I
B  U  I  R  O  L  H  B  S  D
O  D  H  W  I  A  S  J  X  E
E  C  Y  B  K  O  O  G  M  D
T  K  R  E  O  U  U  N  V  N
I  V  N  G  P  C  L  I  M  U
S  S  E  N  N  I  A  L  P  O
J  H  G  N  Z  Q  F  J  H  W
```

JACOB	TESTIFY	CHRIST
UNSHAKEN	WORDS	PLAINNESS
PRIDE	WOUNDED	SOUL

JACOB 1-4

Jacob tells us we should share what we have with others. Draw a picture below of something you have that you could share with others and give to them this week.

I CAN SHARE WITH OTHERS

APRIL 8-14

In Jacob chapter 5, we learn of the Allegory of the Olive Tree, which represents the Lord's dealings with the House of Israel and the Gentiles. As you read the chapter with your family or primary class, match the symbol to it's meaning.

LORD OF THE VINEYARD

PROPHETS

VINEYARD

GENTILES/THOSE WHO HAVEN'T MADE COVENANTS WITH THE LORD

SERVANTS

WORKS OF MEN

TAME OLIVE TREE

JOINING THE HOUSE OF ISRAEL

WILD OLIVE TREE

NOURISHING OTHERS TO RECEIVE BLESSINGS OF SALVATION

GOOD & BAD FRUIT

JESUS CHRIST

DECAY

THE WORLD

GRAFTING

HOUSE OF ISRAEL/GOD'S COVENANT PEOPLE

PRUNING, DIGGING, DUNGING

APOSTASY & WICKEDNESS

BURNING THE VINEYARD

END OF THE WORLD/JUDGEMENT OF GOD

We learn in the story of the Olive Tree, that the Lord wants his servants to cut off the branches with bad fruit and graft in branches with good fruit. On the tree below, cross out the bad fruit and draw some more good fruit on the tree. Why does the Lord want to care for a tree that is decaying?

THE LORD CARES FOR HIS PEOPLE

APRIL 15-21

In Enos, we read about Enos going out to hunt in the forest and praying to God for himself, his brethren the Nephites, and the Lamanites. In the bubbles below, draw or write things you could pray for. Think about Enos and how he prayed not only for himself but for others.

ENOS-WORDS OF MORMON

Mormon followed the direction of the spirit and included the small plates of Nephi in his record. If he hadn't made that choice, we wouldn't have all of the material we have studied so far this year (as the first 116 pages of Joseph Smith's translation was lost). Complete the maze below. Pick the correct path.

I CAN BLESS OTHERS WHEN I LISTEN TO THE HOLY GHOST

APRIL 22-28

In Mosiah 2:17, King Benjamin teaches the importance of serving others. When we serve others, we are serving God. Fill in the missing words from this important scripture verse below.

AND BEHOLD, I TELL YOU THESE THINGS THAT YE MAY LEARN _____; THAT YE MAY _____ THAT WHEN YE ARE IN THE _____ OF YOUR _____ BEINGS YE ARE ____ IN THE SERVICE OF YOUR ____

LEARN   GOD   FELLOW   WISDOM   ONLY   SERVICE

MOSIAH 1-3

King Benjamin spoke to his people. The people brought their families to the temple and pitched their tents facing the temple. Draw a picture below of King Benjamin teaching the people.

KING BENJAMIN TAUGHT IMPORTANT TRUTHS

APRIL 29-MAY 5

CIRCLE THE DAYS YOU READ THIS WEEK: MON TUES WED THUR FRI SAT SUN

In Mosiah 4:1–3, 10, we learn that repentance brings us joy. We can repent because of the Atonement. Color the steps of repentance below.

MOSIAH 4-6

King Benjamin taught us to watch our thoughts and actions. He also asked us to take upon us the name of Christ and to make covenants with Him. Complete the word search below with words from this week's lesson.

```
C  Y  J  T  N  T  S  Z  H  T  S  C
E  Q  G  P  P  W  O  R  D  S  Q  H
B  Z  B  G  O  I  T  E  E  A  V  A
Y  A  P  T  Q  Y  D  P  E  G  J  N
T  L  Q  N  B  W  G  E  D  T  M  G
W  A  T  C  H  F  A  N  S  H  K  E
S  V  O  I  H  V  O  T  E  O  D  E
T  N  H  E  A  R  T  L  R  U  G  Y
N  S  I  N  Z  Y  A  Q  A  G  X  Y
W  I  Z  S  H  H  A  F  P  H  N  R
N  C  G  F  S  W  M  H  A  T  K  T
Q  C  O  V  E  N  A  N  T  S  O  M
```

SIN	WATCH	THOUGHTS
WORDS	DEEDS	CHANGE
HEART	COVENANTS	REPENT

MAY 6-12

In Mosiah 10:10–11, we learn an important lesson. Crack the code below to get the message.

CRACK THE CODE

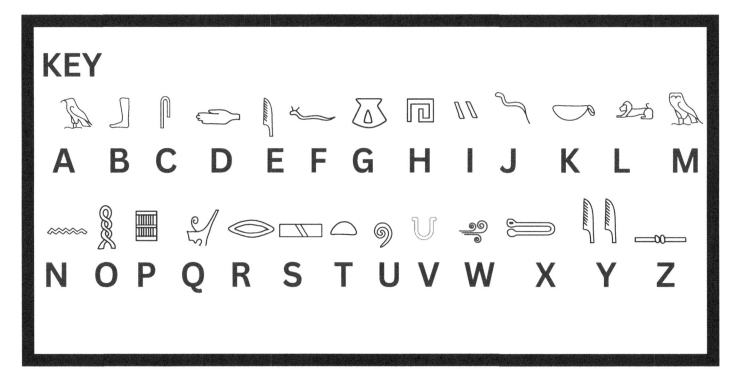

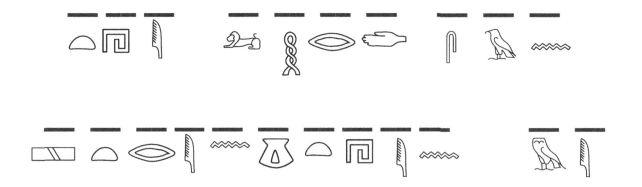

MOSIAH 7-10

In Mosiah 8:16–18, we learn about prophets, seers, and revelators. What are some things we have learned from our prophet and apostles? "Follow the prophet" below by writing or drawing some of his counsel on the footprints.

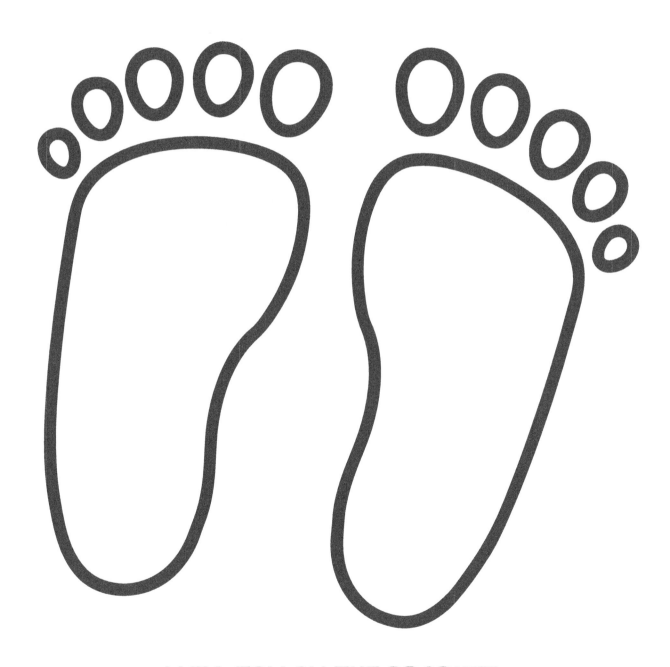

I WILL FOLLOW THE PROPHET

MAY 13-19

In Mosiah 13:11–24, Abinadi teaches that the commandments must be written upon our hearts. Complete the maze below.

I CAN OBEY GOD'S COMMANDMENTS

START

MOSIAH 11-17

In this week's reading, we learn about the courageous prophet Abinadi. As you read, match the correct passage below to the corresponding picture.

REPENT!

KING NOAH WAS A WICKED, LAZY KING

ABINADI WAS GOD'S PROPHET WHO TOLD KING NOAH AND HIS PEOPLE TO REPENT

KING NOAH'S PRIESTS TRIED TRICKING ABINADI WITH THEIR QUESTIONS, BUT THEY COULDN'T

ALMA WAS THE ONLY KING'S PRIEST TO BELIEVE ABINADI. HE RAN AWAY AND HID SO HE WOULDN'T BE KILLED

ABINADI WOULDN'T DENY HIS FAITH AND ALL HE HAD PREACHED, SO HE WAS BURNED

KING NOAH'S FOLLOWERS BURNED HIM, AS ABINADI PROPHESIED

MAY 20-26

Read Mosiah 18:8–10 and Doctrine and Covenants 20:37 and learn about the covenants we make when we are baptized. Fill in the blanks below with one of the words listed.

WHAT I PROMISE

I WILL FOLLOW _____

I WILL _____ OTHERS

I WILL STAND AS A _____ OF GOD

I WILL SERVE GOD & _____ HIS COMMANDMENTS

WITNESS   KEEP   JESUS   HELP

HEAVENLY FATHER PROMISES

HE WILL _____ ME

HE WILL GIVE ME THE _____ OF THE HOLY GHOST

HE WILL GIVE ME ETERNAL _____

FORGIVE   GIFT   LIFE

MOSIAH 18-24

In Mosiah 24:8–17, we learn that God can make our burdens light. Talk with your family or primary class about what that means. Below, color all the words that rhyme with "light."

RHYME TIME - WORDS THAT RHYME WITH "LIGHT"

RIGHT   LIME   KITE   FRIGHT

LIE   BITE   LET   SUN

GOODNIGHT   MIGHT   DARK   FIGHT

MOTE   LIKE   HEIGHT   LIT

MAY 27-JUNE 2

CIRCLE THE DAYS YOU READ THIS WEEK: MON TUES WED THUR FRI SAT SUN

In Mosiah 27:8–37, we read about the conversion of Alma the Younger. See how many words you can make from the words, "Alma repented and changed."

ALMA REPENTED & CHANGED

HOW MANY WORDS CAN YOU MAKE USING THE LETTERS FROM WORDS ABOVE "ALMA REPENTED & CHANGED"?

_____   _____

_____   _____

_____   _____

_____   _____

_____   _____

_____   _____

_____   _____

I CAN REPENT
& BE FORGIVEN

MOSIAH 25-28

In Mosiah 27:8–24, we read about Alma asking his people to fast and pray for Alma the Younger. What other scripture stories can you think of where the people fasted? Is there someone you and your family could fast together for? Color the pictures below and learn more about fasting.

If you are healthy and when you feel ready, you can begin to fast.

Fast Sunday at church is usually the first Sunday of the month.

When fasting, you skip eating & drinking (usually 2 meals).

Pick something or someone to fast for and say a prayer before, during, and after fast.

The money you would have spent on meals during your fast can be given as a fast offering to help those in need.

Look for the blessings and miracles fasting brings.

JUNE 3-9

CIRCLE THE DAYS YOU READ THIS WEEK: MON TUES WED THUR FRI SAT SUN

In Alma 1:2–9, we learn about a false teacher who came among the people. Complete the crossword puzzle below to learn more about this story.

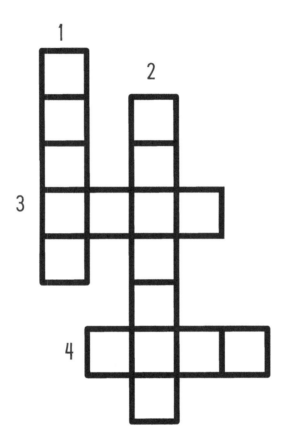

DOWN

1-NAME OF FALSE TEACHER WHO BEGAN PREACHING LIES

2-FALSE TEACHER TOLD PEOPLE, "THEY NEED NOT FEAR NOR _____" BECAUSE EVERYONE WOULD BE SAVED. (SEE ALMA 1:4)

ACROSS

3-GIDEON WAS A RIGHTEOUS MAN WHO DID _____ GOD'S COMMANDS & DEFENDED GOD'S CHURCH AND WAS KILLED BY FALSE TEACHER

4-NAME OF CHIEF JUDGE

MOSIAH 29-ALMA 4

In Alma 4:8–20, we learn that Alma stepped down as Chief Judge among the people so he could go and share his testimony with the people to help bring them back to Christ. What is a testimony? Color the foundations of a testimony below. How is growing your testimony like taking care of a garden?

GOD LIVES & LOVES ME

JESUS ATONED FOR MY SINS

THIS IS GOD'S TRUE CHURCH

THE CHURCH IS LED BY A LIVING PROPHET

A TESTIMONY IS LIKE A GARDEN

JUNE 10-16

In Alma 5:14–33, Alma asks a lot of great questions we can ask ourselves to make sure we are staying close to the Savior. Alma asks if we have had "a mighty change" in our hearts. Write or draw in the heart what you can do to keep close to the Savior. Examples could include being grateful for what you have & not coveting, putting things of God first, speaking kindly of others, sharing, etc.

I CAN HAVE A CHANGE OF HEART & STAY CLOSE TO THE SAVIOR BY:

ALMA 5-7

Read Alma 5:14. What can you do this week to have the Savior's image in your countenance? Draw a picture of what you can do in the mirror below.

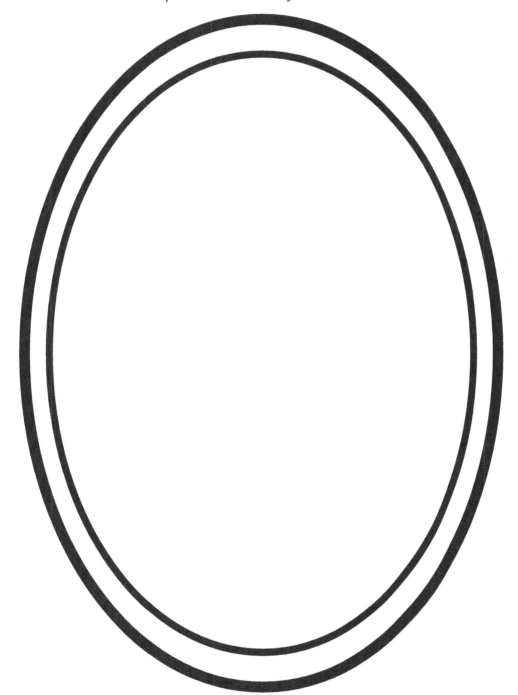

I HAVE THE SAVIOR'S IMAGE IN MY COUNTENANCE

JUNE 17-23

In Alma 8:18–22, we learn how Amulek was a good friend to Alma. What are some things you can do to be a good friend? Write or draw the ways in the circles below. Color the two friends.

I CAN BE A GOOD FRIEND BY...

ALMA 8-12

In this week's reading, we learn about Alma, Amulek, and eventually Zeezrom sharing their testimonies. You can be a missionary now, too, by sharing your testimony with others. In the maze below, help the missionary find his way to those waiting to hear the gospel.

I CAN SHARE THE GOSPEL OF CHRIST

JUNE 24-30

In Alma 13:1–2, 16, we learn how the priesthood power brings us closer to Christ. In the word search below, find words that show ways the priesthood is used in our lives.

PRIESTHOOD POWER BRINGS ME CLOSER TO CHRIST

```
Z  R  S  P  O  U  S  O  F  P  P  N
W  C  A  L  L  I  N  G  H  R  O  O
C  Z  C  J  E  O  Q  G  V  I  P  R
L  B  R  V  S  P  J  P  T  E  T  D
S  J  A  N  N  J  L  A  R  S  E  I
Z  N  M  V  E  I  M  B  Q  T  M  N
Y  H  E  X  B  R  M  A  F  H  P  A
D  Y  N  Z  I  M  L  P  N  O  L  N
S  M  T  F  Y  G  S  T  J  O  E  C
C  J  N  C  M  P  O  I  A  D  S  E
U  O  X  J  K  F  A  S  C  C  T  S
C  E  M  Y  O  M  J  M  X  K  M  O
```

BAPTISM	CONFIRMATION	SICK
CALLING	SACRAMENT	PRIESTHOOD
ORDINANCES	TEMPLES	

ALMA 13-16

In this week's reading, we learn about the righteous being burned and Alma and Amulek being freed from prison miraculously. Match each event to its correct picture below.

WICKED PEOPLE THREW WOMEN & CHILDREN WHO BELIEVED THE WORD OF GOD INTO A FIRE TO DIE

ALMA AND AMULEK PUT IN PRISON

ALMA AND AMULEK TIED UP & TAKEN TO CHIEF JUDGE

PRION WALLS FELL & EVERYONE INSIDE WAS KILLED EXCEPT ALMA & AMULEK

WICKED PEOPLE IN AMMONIHAH KILLED BY LAMANITES

ZEEZROM REPENTS, IS HEALED, AND IS BAPTIZED

JULY 1-7

In this week's lesson, we learn about the sons of Mosiah going to preach the gospel to the Lamanites. Pretend you are a missionary and write or draw some things you would tell people on the doors below.

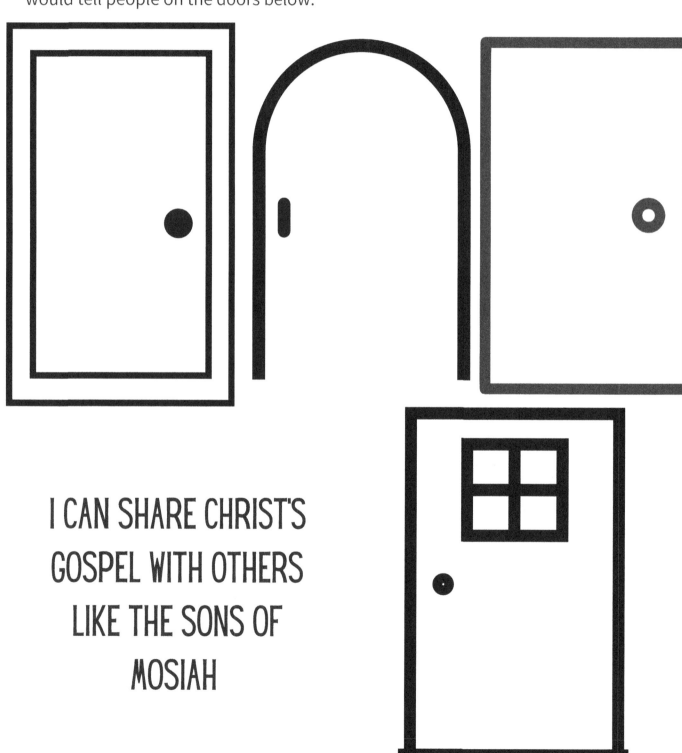

I CAN SHARE CHRIST'S GOSPEL WITH OTHERS LIKE THE SONS OF MOSIAH

ALMA 17-22

In Alma chapter 17, we read that Ammon becomes a servant of King Lamoni and is responsible for watching over his sheep. Color the pictures below that tell about this story.

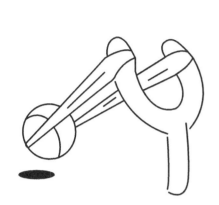

AMMON KILLED SOME OF THOSE TRYING TO STEAL THE KING'S FLOCKS WITH STONES & A SLING.

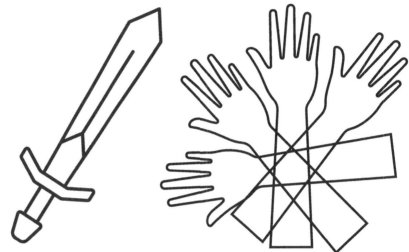

THE OTHER THIEVES TRIED TO KILL AMMON, BUT HE CUT THEIR ARMS OFF WITH HIS SWORD.

THE ARMS THAT WERE CUT OFF WERE TAKEN TO SHOW THE KING WHAT HAD BEEN DONE. THE KING IS THEN CONVERTED AFTER AMMON TEACHES HIM.

AMMON SAVED THE KING'S SHEEP

JULY 8-14

CIRCLE THE DAYS YOU READ THIS WEEK: MON TUES WED THUR FRI SAT SUN

In Alma 24:17-18, the Anti-Nephi-Lehies, buried all their weapons of war. They did this as a testimony to God that they would never use weapons to shed another person's blood. Color the picture below. You can draw a picture of you next to the shovel & pretend you are burying your weapons.

THE LORD BLESSES ME AS I WORK TO KEEP MY PROMISES TO HIM

ALMA 23-29

In this week's reading, we can see a great change that happened to the Lamanites once they took the name Anti-Nephi-Lehi upon them. We read in Alma 24:7–10 what helped them change. Color all the words below that rhyme with "repent."

RHYME TIME - WORDS THAT RHYME WITH "REPENT"

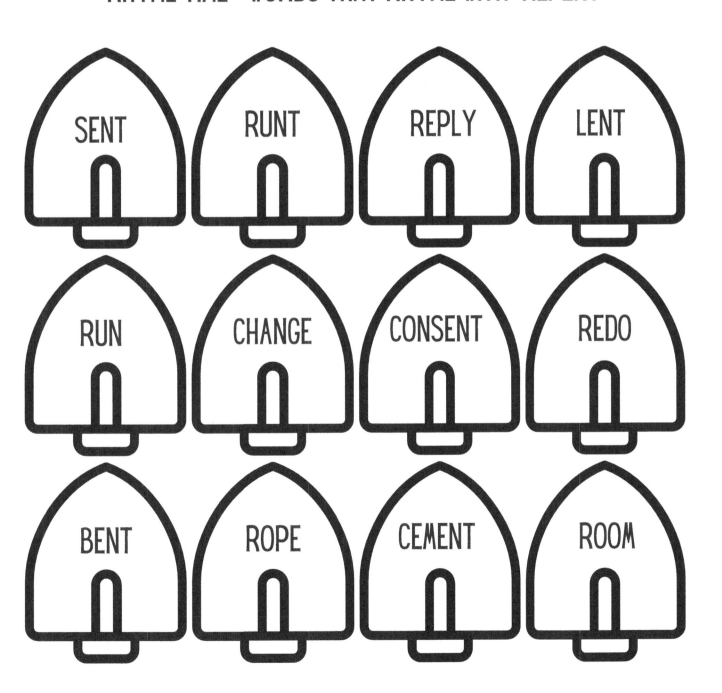

SENT   RUNT   REPLY   LENT

RUN   CHANGE   CONSENT   REDO

BENT   ROPE   CEMENT   ROOM

JULY 15-21

CIRCLE THE DAYS YOU READ THIS WEEK: MON TUES WED THUR FRI SAT SUN

In Alma 30:44, Alma testifies to Korihor, a false teacher who came among the people. What does Alma say to him? Crack the code below to find out.

CRACK THE CODE

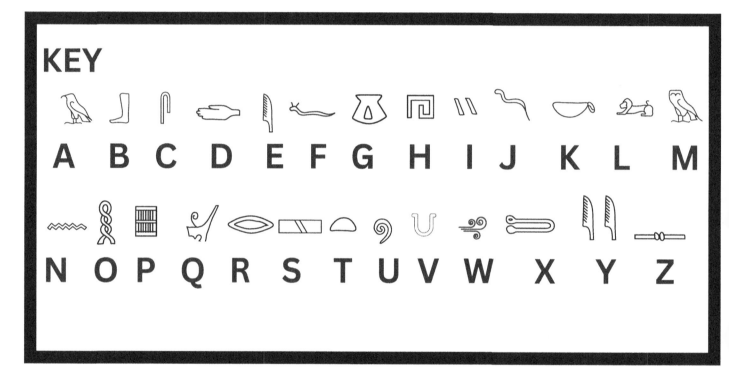

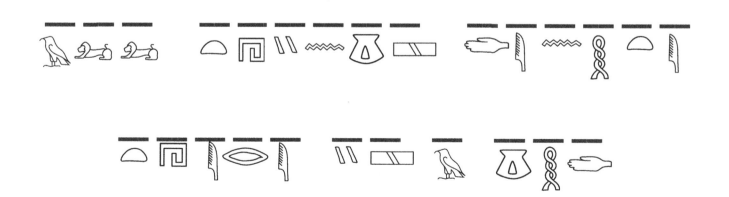

ALMA 30-31

In Alma 31, Alma and some missionaries went to preach to the Zoramites. The Zoramites would take turns standing on a tall tower and repeat the same prayer. Listed below the "rameumptom" on this page are some of the Zoramites false beliefs. Match the false belief with the opposite, true doctrine of Christ that Alma taught.

ZORAMITE'S BELIEFS

DOCTRINE OF CHRIST

GOD IS A SPIRIT

THERE WOULD BE NO CHRIST

ZORAMITES THOUGHT ONLY THEY WOULD BE SAVED

ZORAMITES ALL SAID THE EXACT SAME PRAYER

AFTER THEY PRAYED, THEY WENT HOME & DID NOT PRAY OR TALK OF GOD AGAIN THE REST OF THE WEEK

THEY LOVED RICHES AND WORLDLY THINGS & BRAGGED ABOUT THEIR RICHES

CHRIST WOULD COME AND ATONE FOR THE SINS OF ALL MANKIND

WE SHOULD PRAY ALWAYS & BE AN EXAMPLE OF CHRIST EVERY DAY

WE SHOULD PUT THE THINGS OF GOD FIRST

EVERYONE CAN BE SAVED THROUGH CHRIST'S ATONEMENT

GOD HAS A BODY

GOD DOESN'T WANT US TO JUST REPEAT REPETITIONS IN OUR PRAYERS, BUT TO SHARE THINGS ON OUR HEART

JULY 22-28

In Alma 32:27, Alma teaches that if we show even just a little faith, our testimonies will begin to grow. See how many words you can make from the words "exercise a particle of faith."

EXERCISE A PARTICLE OF FAITH

HOW MANY WORDS CAN YOU MAKE USING THE LETTERS FROM WORDS ABOVE "EXERCISE A PARTICLE OF FAITH"?

_____   _____

_____   _____

_____   _____

_____   _____

_____   _____

_____   _____

_____   _____

_____

In Alma 32:28–43, Alma compares faith to a seed & tells us we need to nourish our faith for it to grow. Color the picture below.

MY TESTIMONY GROWS AS I NOURISH IT

JULY 29-AUGUST 4

CIRCLE THE DAYS YOU READ THIS WEEK: MON TUES WED THUR FRI SAT SUN

In Alma 37:6–7, we learn that by "small and simple things are great things brought to pass." Match the small item below with the big thing it makes happen. What big things happen when we follow simple commandments?

ALMA 36-38

In Alma 37:38–47, we learn about the Liahona and how it was a guide for Lehi and his family and worked according to their faith. Similarly, today we have the scriptures as a guide. Complete the maze below and find your way from the scriptures to the Savior.

AUGUST 5-11

In Alma 39:1, we learn that Shiblon was a good example to his brother Corianton. Draw how you can be a good example to a sibling or friends in the box below.

I CAN BE A CHRISTLIKE EXAMPLE

ALMA 39-42

In Alma 40, we learn more about what happens when we die. Complete the word search below with words from the reading.

```
G  P  J  U  D  G  E  M  E  N  T
T  J  S  T  B  O  D  Y  H  I  C
U  H  T  A  S  B  I  R  R  D  O
D  R  B  A  L  Q  J  I  L  J  P
P  O  H  F  O  E  P  R  Q  F  A
L  L  P  R  I  S  O  N  R  J  R
L  H  D  H  Q  W  Y  L  P  W  A
I  R  E  R  T  W  Y  F  O  I  D
V  I  A  T  L  W  W  O  T  B  I
E  D  T  C  O  O  P  D  H  R  S
M  Q  H  G  Y  S  F  B  K  N  E
```

SPIRIT	WORLD	DEATH
PARADISE	PRISON	JUDGEMENT
BODY	LIVE	

AUGUST 12-18

In Alma 46:11–16, Captain Moroni made a "Title of Liberty" to remind the people why they needed to protect their freedom and to encourage the people to help defend their freedom against Amalickiah. Below make your own "Title of Liberty" by writing or drawing on the flag.

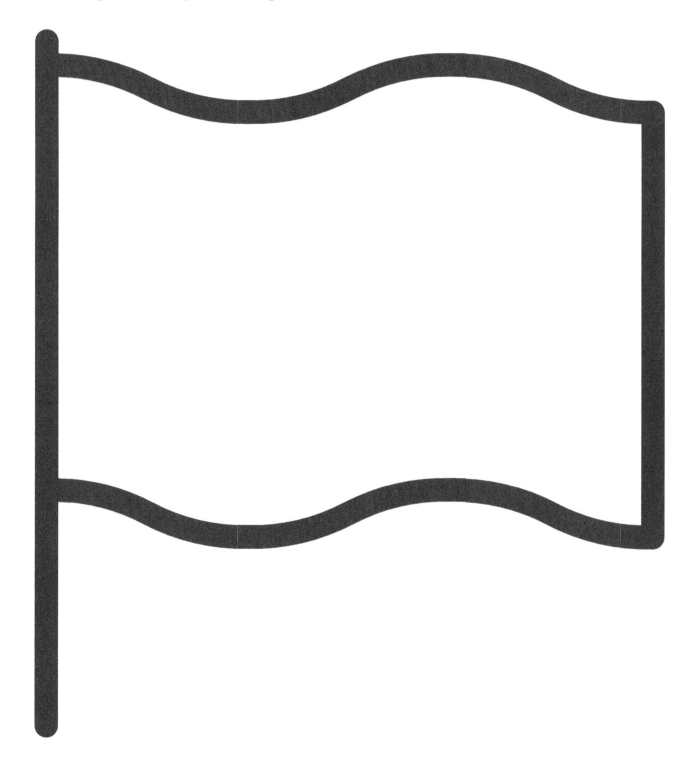

ALMA 43-52

In Alma 48:7–9, we learn some of the ways the Nephites fortified their cities. How can we fortify and protect our homes spiritually against Satan? Write or draw the ways in the home below.

WE CAN SPIRITUALLY PROTECT OUR HOMES

AUGUST 19-25

In Alma 53:20–21; 56:47–48; 57:26, we learn about Helaman and his army of young, righteous soldiers. Below, color the words with qualities that describe the soldiers.

I CAN BE FAITHFUL TO GOD LIKE THE STRIPLING WARRIORS

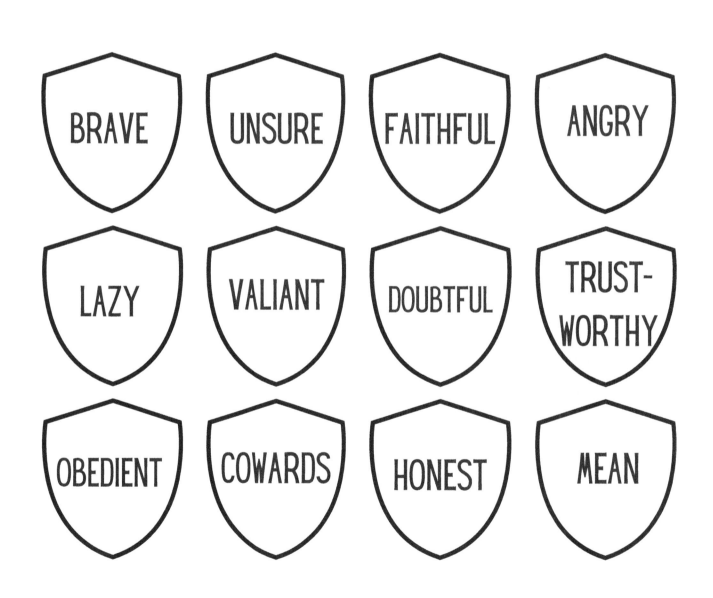

HOW MANY WARRIORS WERE THERE?_____ HOW MANY DIED? _____

In Alma 56:48, we learn what the Army of Helaman soldiers said about their mothers. Crack the code below to read their message.

CRACK THE CODE

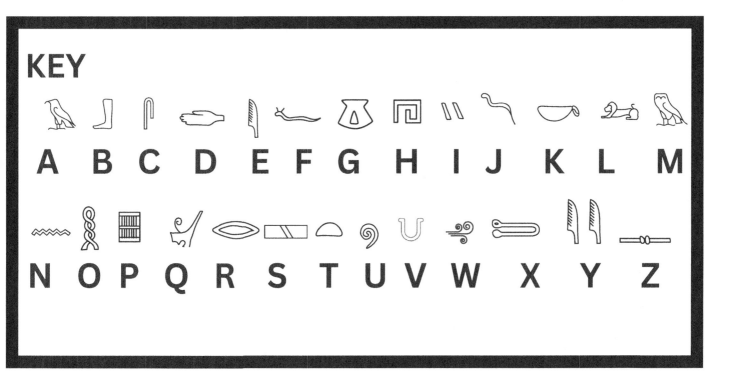

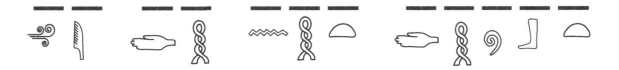

In Helaman 3:24, 33–34; 4:11–15, we see a pattern that is shown throughout the Book of Mormon called the "Pride Cycle." The people are righteous and begin to prosper and then pride and sin creeps in and they make choices that causes suffering and destruction. They then repent and humble themselves and become a righteous people again. Color the pictures below representing the pride cycle.

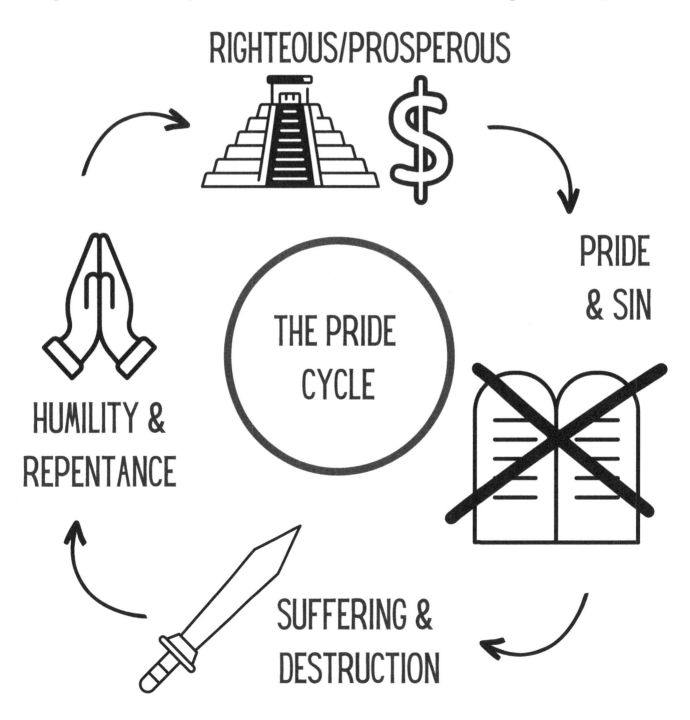

HELAMAN 1-6

In Helaman 5, we learn about Helaman's sons and their mission to the Nephites and the Lamanites. Complete the cross-word puzzle below to learn more about their mission.

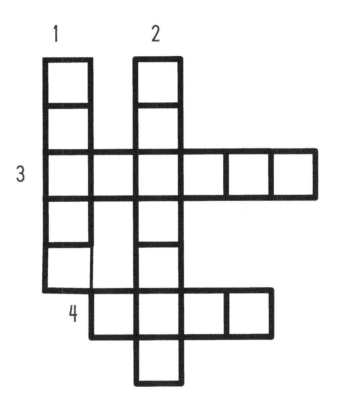

DOWN

1-HELAMAN'S SONS LEHI AND _____ WENT TO PREACH THE GOSPEL. THEY PREACHED WITH SUCH POWER & AUTHORITY THAT THEY DID CONVERT AND BAPTIZE 8,000 LAMANITES

2-IN VERSE 30, A VOICE LIKE A _____ BEGAN TO SPEAK

ACROSS

3-HELAMAN'S SONS WENT TO THE LAND OF NEPHI AND WERE THROWN IN _____

4-THE LAMANITES WENT INTO THE PRISON TO KILL HELAMAN'S SONS BUT COULDN'T BECAUSE THEY _____PROTECTED BY FIRE.

SEPTEMBER 2-8

In Helaman 5, the word "remember" is used by Helaman to teach his sons to remember to keep the commandments. See how many words you can make from the phrase, "remember to keep the commandments".

REMEMBER TO KEEP THE COMMANDMENTS

HOW MANY WORDS CAN YOU MAKE USING THE LETTERS FROM THE WORDS "REMEMBER TO KEEP THE COMMANDMENTS"?

_____   _____

_____   _____

_____   _____

_____   _____

_____   _____

_____   _____

_____

DON'T FORGET!

In Helaman 8:13–23, we are reminded of the many prophets who testified of Christ. The prophet leads us to Jesus. On the foot prints below, write or draw ways the prophet helps you come unto Christ.

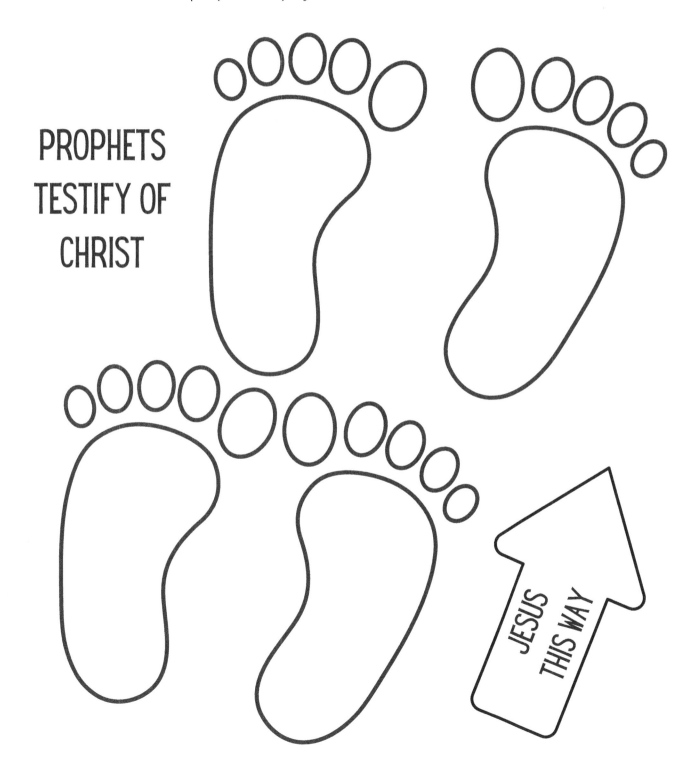

PROPHETS TESTIFY OF CHRIST

JESUS THIS WAY

SEPTEMBER 9-15

CIRCLE THE DAYS YOU READ THIS WEEK: MON TUES WED THUR FRI SAT SUN

In Helaman 16, we see Samuel was protected from the stones and arrows the Nephites threw and shot at him when he was preaching on the wall. Count the arrows below.

HOW MANY DO YOU COUNT?

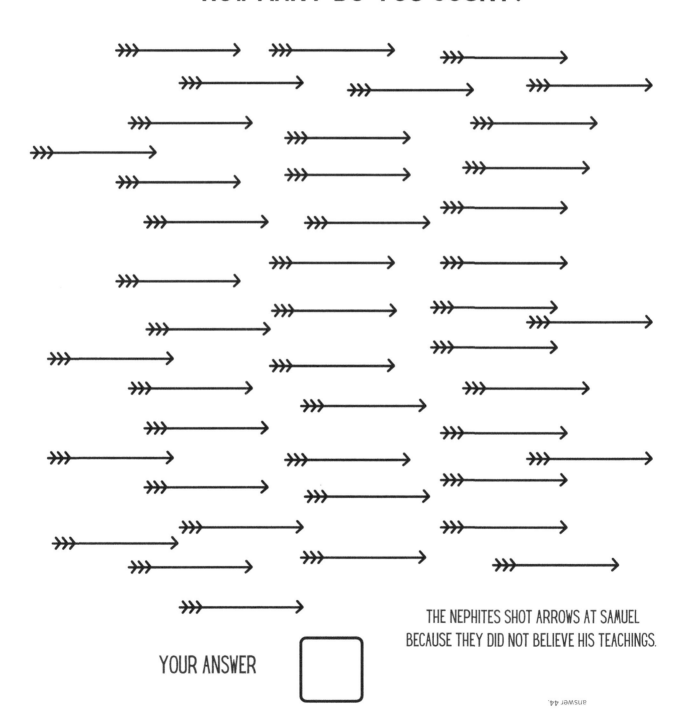

YOUR ANSWER

THE NEPHITES SHOT ARROWS AT SAMUEL
BECAUSE THEY DID NOT BELIEVE HIS TEACHINGS.

answer 44.

HELAMAN 13-16

In Helaman 13:2–5, we learn that Samuel spoke the things that God put in his heart. God speaks to us through the Holy Ghost. Color the ways below that the Holy Ghost can communicate God's message to us.

THOUGHTS THAT STAY ON YOUR MIND

SOMETHING YOU FEEL IN YOUR HEART

A WHISPER OR VOICE YOU HEAR IN YOUR MIND

A FEELING THAT YOU SHOULDN'T DO SOMETHING

A DESIRE TO FOLLOW THE COMMANDMENTS

A HAPPY, PEACEFUL FEELING THAT SOMETHING IS A GOOD CHOICE

GOD CAN SPEAK TO ME THROUGH THE HOLY GHOST

SEPTEMBER 16-22

In 3 Nephi 1:4–15, 19–21, we read that the sign was given that Christ was born. There was a night without darkness and a new star appeared. Color the picture below.

THE NEPHITES SAW A NEW STAR APPEAR WHEN JESUS WAS BORN

3 NEPHI 1-7

In 3 Nephi 2:11–12, we learn that the righteous gathered together to be protected from the growing number of Gadianton robbers. There is strength in unity. We can find strength in our families and with other church members. Help the lost person below find his way back to his family.

SEPTEMBER 23-29

CIRCLE THE DAYS YOU READ THIS WEEK: MON TUES WED THUR FRI SAT SUN

In 3 Nephi 11, Jesus Christ showed himself to the people of Nephi. He let them feel the nail prints in his hands and feet. Draw a picture of what you think think this looked like.

JESUS CHRIST VISITED THE NEPHITES

3 NEPHI 8-11

In 3 Nephi chapters 8 & 9, we learn about the events that happened to the Nephites after the Savior was resurrected. Match the description to it's picture below.

TIMELINE OF EVENTS TO THE RESURRECTED CHRIST VISITING THE NEPHITES

GREAT DOUBTING AMONG PEOPLE THAT CHRIST WOULD COME

GREAT STORM, EARTHQUAKES, FIRES, CITIES SUNK, WICKED DESTROYED

GREAT DARKNESS FOR THREE DAYS

THE PEOPLE HEAR A VOICE THREE TIMES & FINALLY UNDERSTAND IT IS GOD INTRODUCING HIS SON & JESUS CHRIST DESCENDS. THE PEOPLE FEEL HIS NAIL PRINTS

JESUS TEACHES ABOUT BAPTISM

SEPTEMBER 30-OCTOBER 6

In 3 Nephi 12:14–16, Jesus teaches the people to let their light shine. Below write or draw ways you can let your light shine. Color the candle.

I WILL LET MY LIGHT SHINE

3 NEPHI 12-16

In this week's reading, Jesus teaches doctrine similar to what He taught at the Sermon on the Mount in the bible. Find words related to the reading in the word search below.

```
Y  S  E  R  U  S  A  E  R  T  I  D
F  B  L  Q  B  Q  D  P  G  N  J  U
U  S  U  P  D  F  O  O  L  I  S  H
V  R  R  P  S  R  L  C  U  K  E  C
E  A  A  D  W  A  N  K  J  I  W  W
Y  G  O  Q  E  N  N  H  J  E  I  U
B  E  A  T  I  T  U  D  E  S  M  E
R  A  H  D  I  F  K  K  E  Q  K  F
E  Y  J  E  S  U  S  I  P  C  O  I
C  Y  T  Q  M  D  N  F  O  Y  P  W
K  O  K  M  Z  T  L  R  Z  U  H  M
P  I  U  T  A  U  G  H  T  K  T  Y
```

JESUS	TAUGHT	BEATITUDES
PRAY	TREASURES	ROCK
SAND	WISE	FOOLISH

OCTOBER 7-13

In 3 Nephi 17:24-25, we read that angels came down and ministered to the children. Color the wings below that are synonyms (mean almost the same thing) with "angel."

WORDS THAT ARE SYNONYMS WITH "ANGEL"

FABLE CHERUB MESSENGER UNKIND

HAZEL REBEL SAINT FULL

DEVIL FEEBLE BAGEL PROCLAIMER

KIND TANGLE LIFESAVER HEAVENLY

3 NEPHI 17-19

In 3 Nephi 18:1–12, Jesus teaches about the sacrament. Below draw what you can think about during the sacrament.

I CAN THINK OF JESUS WHEN I TAKE THE SACRAMENT

OCTOBER 14-20

In 3 Nephi 24:7–12, we learn about the importance of paying our tithing. What are we promised when we pay our tithing? Crack the code below.

CRACK THE CODE

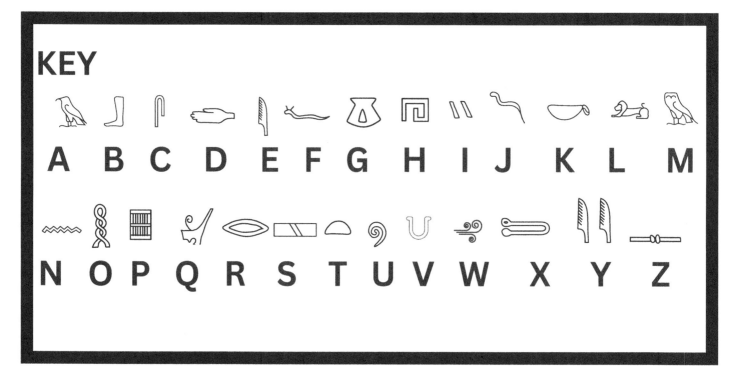

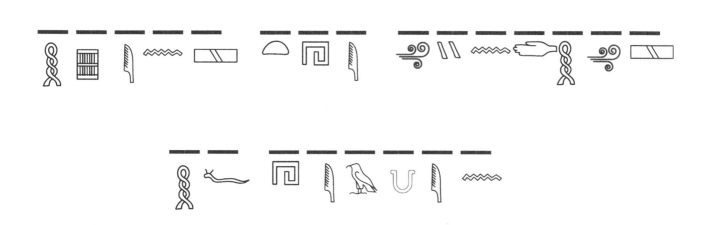

3 NEPHI 20-26

In 3 Nephi 25:5–6, we learn about turning "the hearts of the fathers to the children" through family history & temple work. Draw a picture of your family below.

FAMILIES CAN BE TOGETHER FOREVER

In 3 Nephi 27:3–8, we learn about the name of Christ's church. Color the picture below.

I belong to the

of Jesus Christ

3 NEPHI 27-4 NEPHI

In 3 Nephi 28:1–11, the Savior asks each of His disciples what they desire. Solve the clues below to complete the cross word puzzle.

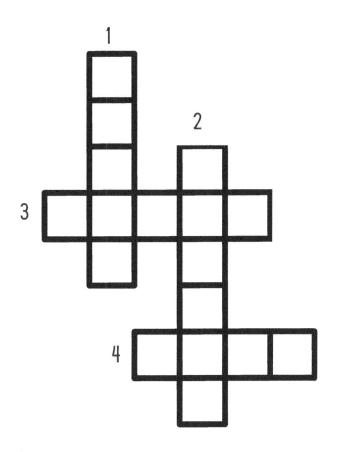

DOWN

1-ALL BUT HOW MANY ASKED FOR THE SAME THING? (VS. 2)

2-JESUS TOLD THESE DISCIPLES WHEN THEY WERE 72 YEARS OLD THEY COULD COME LIVE WITH HIM IN _____

ACROSS

3-THE REMAINING DISCIPLES WISHED TO _____ TASTE DEATH (VS. 7)

4-JESUS TOLD THE DISCIPLES THEY WILL COME TO HIS KINGDOM AND FIND_____ (VS. 3)

OCTOBER 28-NOVEMBER 3

In Mormon 1:1–3, we read about the special task Mormon was given. See how many words you can make from the letters in the words, "The Book of Mormon" below.

THE BOOK OF MORMON

HOW MANY WORDS CAN YOU MAKE USING THE LETTERS FROM WORDS "THE BOOK OF MORMON"?

In Mormon 3:3, 9, we see the Lord had blessed the Nephites but they were ungrateful. On the leaves below, write or draw what you are grateful for.

I AM GRATEFUL

NOVEMBER 4-10

In Mormon 7:8–10, we read that the Bible and the Book of Mormon testify of Christ. Read the statements below and draw a line to either the Bible or Book of Mormon or both, depending on where the story and doctrine is found.

THE HOLY BIBLE

THE BOOK OF MORMON

TESTIFIES OF JESUS' RESURRECTION

TELLS THE STORY OF QUEEN ESTHER & HER COURAGE

TEACHES THE IMPORTANCE & POWER OF CHRIST'S ATONEMENT

TELLS THE STORY OF THE 2,000 STRIPLING WARRIORS

TESTIFIES OF JESUS' BIRTH

TELLS OF MIRACLES CHRIST AND HIS PROPHETS PERFORMED

MORMON 7-9

In Mormon 8:1–7, we read that the Nephites were destroyed and Moroni is alone. All his friends and family were killed by the Lamanites. Moroni was obedient and finished writing the record of what happened to his people. Even though Moroni was all alone, he still chose to keep the commandments. Draw a picture below of Moroni.

MORONI IS LEFT ALONE TO FINISH THE RECORD

NOVEMBER 11-17

In this week's reading we learn about the Jaredites, who lived at the time of the Tower of Babel. They prayed to the Lord that their language would not be changed so they could still understand each other. The Lord answered their prayer. Color the picture below.

HEAVENLY FATHER HEARS & ANSWERS MY PRAYERS

ETHER 1-5

The Jaredites were commanded to build barges to come to the promised land. The Brother of Jared molten 16 small, clear stones and asked the Lord to touch them so they could have light in their barges. Complete the maze below.

NOVEMBER 18-24

CIRCLE THE DAYS YOU READ THIS WEEK: MON TUES WED THUR FRI SAT SUN

In Ether 6:1–12, we read about the Jaredites journey across the ocean. There were many storms and big waves, but they praised God and made it safely to the promised land. How can God help you when you are scared? Spot the differences in the pictures below.

SPOT THE 5 DIFFERENCES

ETHER 6-11

In Ether 6:12, when the Jaredites arrived to the promised land after being on water for 344 days, they shed tears of joy for the "tender mercies" the Lord had showed them. Complete the word search below with words from this week's reading.

```
C  O  M  A  V  G  S  V  J  B  Q
P  F  H  H  S  E  I  C  R  E  M
V  P  J  A  R  E  D  O  S  M  T
P  R  E  D  N  E  T  D  E  M  Q
J  F  R  Q  Y  H  G  S  N  E  Z
P  R  A  Y  E  D  D  E  O  O  N
F  B  E  R  D  S  H  G  T  R  P
Z  L  N  T  L  P  B  R  S  R  U
A  S  A  V  A  B  Q  A  R  E  S
S  T  U  T  H  W  C  B  D  W  M
H  E  I  P  C  G  T  H  G  I  L
```

BROTHER	JARED	BARGES
STONES	LIGHT	PRAYED
WATER	TENDER	MERCIES

NOVEMBER 25-DECEMBER 1

CIRCLE THE DAYS YOU READ THIS WEEK: MON TUES WED THUR FRI SAT SUN

In Ether 12:6, we learn about faith. Complete the verse below with the missing words.

AND NOW, I, _____, WOULD SPEAK SOMEWHAT CONCERNING THESE THINGS; I WOULD SHOW UNTO THE WORLD THAT _____IS THINGS WHICH ARE _____ FOR AND NOT _____; WHEREFORE, DISPUTE NOT BECAUSE YE _____NOT, FOR YE RECEIVE NO WITNESS UNTIL AFTER THE _____OF YOUR FAITH.

FAITH   SEEN   MORONI   TRIAL   HOPED   SEE

ETHER 12-15

In Ether 12:4, we learn of hope being like an anchor. How do anchors help boats? How is hope like an anchor to our souls? Color the picture below.

HOPE IS LIKE AN ANCHOR TO OUR SOULS

DECEMBER 2-8

In Moroni 4:3 and 5:2, we read the sacrament prayers. Can you say these prayers from memory? What are two of the things the prayer asks us to do? Crack the code below to find out.

CRACK THE CODE

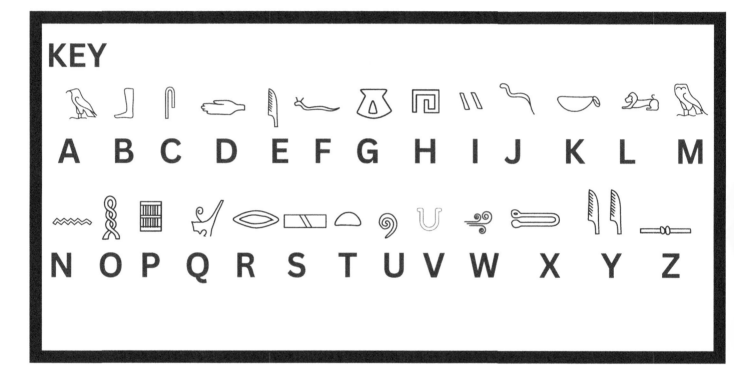

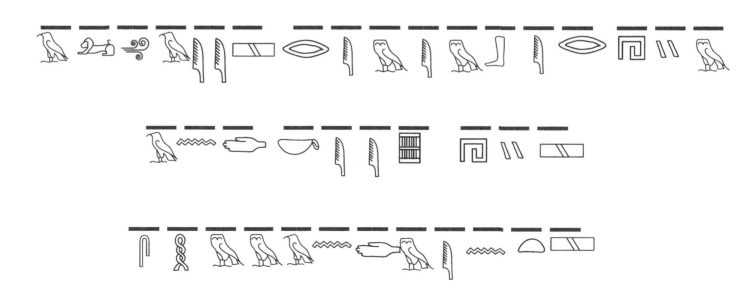

MORONI 1-6

In Moroni 6:4, we read after baptism we should be "nourished by the good word of God." Color the foods below that are nourishing for our bodies. How does the word of God nourish us?

DECEMBER 9-15

In Moroni 7:41, Moroni tells us some things we should hope for. Color the hearts with words that rhyme with "hope" below.

WORDS THAT RHYME WITH "HOPE"

ROPE HOP SOAP HELP

HAIR CAPE MOPE SLOPE

COPE ANTELOPE HAPPY ENVELOPE

HEART TROPHY NOPE FAITH

BELIEVING IN CHRIST GIVES ME HOPE

MORONI 7-9

In Moroni 7:47, we read about charity being the pure love of Christ. Think of something kind you can do for someone this week and draw a picture of it below. Can you think of ways Jesus showed charity?

CHARITY IS THE PURE LOVE OF CHRIST

DECEMBER 16-22

CIRCLE THE DAYS YOU READ THIS WEEK: MON TUES WED THUR FRI SAT SUN

In Moroni chapter 10, Moroni invites us to ask God if the Book of Mormon is true. Match the phrase below with the correct image.

I CAN ASK GOD IF THE BOOK OF MORMON IS TRUE

MORONI FINISHED WRITING
HIS RECORD

MORONI INVITES US TO READ
THE BOOK OF MORMON

ONCE WE READ THE BOOK OF
MORMON, WE SHOULD ASK
GOD IF IT IS TRUE

IF WE ASK WITH FAITH, THE
HOLY GHOST WILL LET US
KNOW THE RECORD IS TRUE

MORONI BURIED THE PLATES
& HIS MORTAL WORK WAS
FINISHED

MORONI 10

In Moroni 10:8–19, we learn about spiritual gifts. What spiritual gifts do you have? You can write some of your gifts on the gift below and color.

I HAVE BEEN GIVEN SPIRITUAL GIFTS

DECEMBER 23-29

The Book of Mormon testifies of Jesus Christ, as stated in 2 Nephi 25:23. Reflect on all you have learned this year & and draw your favorite scripture story or favorite person from the Book of Mormon below.

THE BOOK OF MORMON TESTIFIES OF CHRIST

CHRISTMAS

Finish drawing the picture of the birth of Jesus below.

JESUS CHRIST CAME TO EARTH TO BE OUR SAVIOR

GOAL REFLECTION

How did you do with your spiritual, physical, social, and intellectual goals the past year? Discuss with your family. In space below, write or draw a picture of something you have learned from studying the Book of Mormon this year.

IF YOU ENJOYED THIS BOOK, MAKE SURE TO LEAVE A REVIEW.

CHECK OUT OUR OTHER BOOKS.

FOLLOW US ONLINE!

@LATTER.DAY.DESIGNS

LATTER-DAY DESIGNS

Made in the USA
Las Vegas, NV
07 January 2024

84046648R00063